Amazing life cycles
FISH
by Honor Head

D1103253

An Hachette UK Company
www.hachette.co.uk
Copyright © Octopus Publishing Group Ltd 2013
First published in Great Britain in 2007 by TickTock, an imprint of
Octopus Publishing Group Ltd, Endeavour House, 189 Shaftesbury Avenue, London WC2H 8JY.
www.octopusbooks.co.uk

ISBN 978 1 84898 942 9

Printed and bound in China
10 9 8 7 6 5

With thanks to: Trudi Webb, Sally Morgan and Elizabeth Wiggans
Natural history consultant (2013): Dr. Kim Dennis-Bryan F.Z.S
Publisher: Tim Cook   Cover design: Steve West   Production Controller: Alexandra Bell

Picture credits (t=top; b=bottom; c=centre; l=left; r=right):
FLPA: 5b, 7t, 7b, 8 main, 11b, 12b, 16, 17, 20, 21, 25t, 27b, 28–29 main, 30c. Nature Picture Library: 15cr, 15cl.
NHPA: 14cl, 19b. Shutterstock: OFC, 1, 2, 3, 4tl, 4c, 5t, 6tl, 6b, 8tl, 9t, 9c, 9b, 10tl, 10 main, 11t, 12tl, 13t, 13b, 14tl, 14ct, 14cr, 14b,
15t, 15bl, 15br, 18 main, 19t, 22tl, 23, 24tl, 24b, 25b, 26, 27t, 28tl, 29b, 30tl, 31, OBC.
Superstock: 22c. TickTock image archive: map page 6, 18tl.

Contents

Words that look
bold like this are
in the glossary.

What is a fish?

Many fish are covered in scales that help to protect them.

A fish is an animal that lives in water. All fish have fins, most have **scales**. A fish can breathe underwater using body parts called **gills**. The gills take **oxygen** out of the water and pass it into the fish's body.

Fish use their fins and tail to move through the water.

Fin

Gill cover

Some fish live alone. Others live in big groups called shoals. A shoal can have hundreds or thousands of fish.

Fin

These fish eggs have been attached to an underwater rock by a female fish.

Most fish **reproduce** by laying eggs. The eggs are very small and soft. The female fish usually lays hundreds of eggs in one go.

Sharks are a type of fish. Some sharks, such as the great white shark, give birth to live babies called pups.

A great white shark.

Tail

AMAZING FISH FACT
When great white shark pups are born they are thought to be over a metre long and have sharp teeth, ready for hunting!

Fish habitats

Blue tang fish live on coral reefs. They hide in the reef's holes and cracks at night and when danger is present.

A habitat is the place where a plant or an animal lives. The ocean is a habitat, so are rivers and lakes. Many fish live in the ocean which is **saltwater**. Other types of fish live in **freshwater** ponds or streams.

Fish live in all the world's oceans.

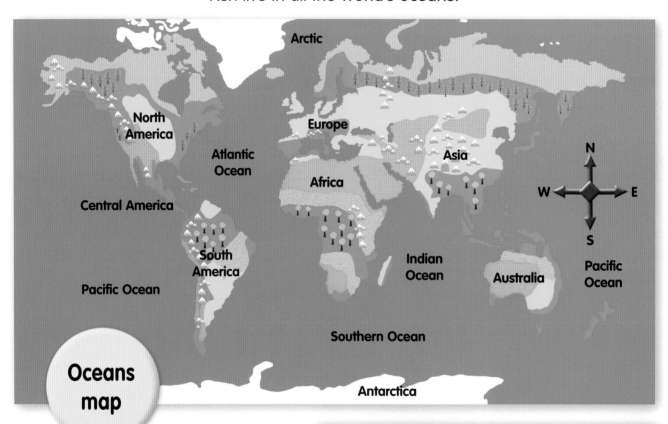

Arctic

North America

Europe

Asia

Atlantic Ocean

Africa

Central America

South America

Indian Ocean

Australia

Pacific Ocean

Pacific Ocean

Southern Ocean

Antarctica

N
W E
S

Oceans map

Some of the most colourful fish live around **coral reefs**. These reefs grow in the shallow waters of warm oceans.

There are lots of coral reefs in the Pacific and Indian Oceans.

Some strange looking fish live at the very bottom of deep oceans where it is cold, dark and there is very little food.

The deepwater fangtooth fish has a huge mouth that helps it catch any fish it can find – even if the fish is the same size as the fangtooth fish!

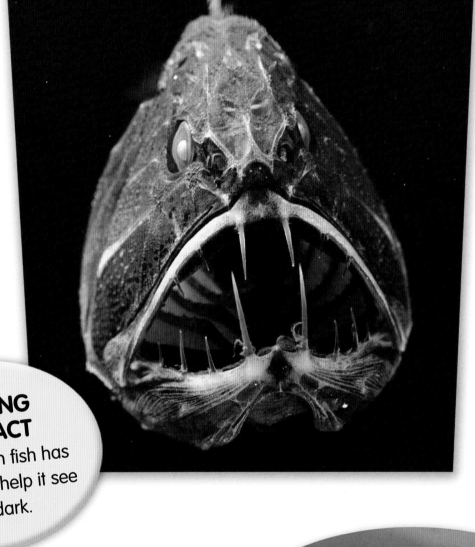

AMAZING FISH FACT
The fangtooth fish has large eyes to help it see in the dark.

The mudskipper is a fish that lives in shallow water in muddy **swamps**. It spends most of its time out of water and can 'walk' using its fins.

Fin

Ocean fish

Ocean fish can be just a few centimetres long, or enormous like the whale shark – the biggest fish in the world! Some ocean fish don't even look like fish, but more like seaweed or stones.

Stonefish live on the ocean floor. They look just like stones and have a nasty sting!

Whale shark

AMAZING FISH FACT
The whale shark can grow to 14 metres long. Unlike most other sharks, it feeds almost entirely on **plankton**.

The leafy seadragon lives in warm oceans around Australia. It hides in seaweed using its leaf-like decorations as **camouflage**.

Many fish that live in coral reefs have bright colours or patterns. They use the reef to help keep them safe from **predators**, such as bigger fish.

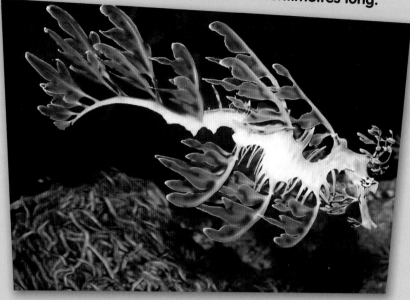

This leafy seadragon is about 45 centimetres long.

Pretend eye

This butterfly fish's black spot looks like an eye. A predator is not sure which end is the right end to attack.

Tomato clownfish

Sea anemone

The tomato clownfish lives on coral reefs hidden from predators among the stinging tentacles of **sea anemones**.

The clownfish's body is covered in a special slime. Scientists believe the slime protects the fish from the anemone's stings.

Freshwater fish

Some freshwater fish live in clear, flowing streams or rivers. Others live in ponds where the water is very still and where lots of weeds grow.

Perch live in rivers and lakes. Females lay 300,000 eggs at one time!

Most catfish live in lakes and rivers. They eat fish, shellfish and any other small creatures they can find. They usually feed at night.

Barbel

AMAZING FISH FACT
Catfish use their long whiskers, or barbels, to feel for food along the bottom of lakes and rivers.

Piranhas live in freshwater rivers in South America.

Piranhas are freshwater fish that eat other fish, insects, seeds and fruit. But sometimes piranhas will eat larger animals!

If the river dries up during a hot time of year, the piranhas are forced to live together in a small amount of water. If a large animal, such as a horse, steps into the water, the hungry piranhas will attack as a group!

Piranhas have razor-sharp teeth!

Mum meets dad

This is a pair of long-nosed butterfly fish. All butterfly fish pair for life.

Most fish reproduce every year. Some fish find a mate and stay together as a pair for life. Other fish have a new partner each year. Many fish **mate** with more than one partner in the same year.

Hammerhead sharks can live in shoals of over 500 sharks. The largest, healthiest females swim in the middle of the shoal.

When they are ready to mate they start shaking their head from side to side. This makes the other females swim to th edges of the shoal.

AMAZING FISH FACT

Sharks live in all the world's oceans. They have been around since before the dinosaurs!

Now the strongest females are the centre of attention and are sure to get a mate.

The angelfish pair in this photo are guarding their eggs.

The angelfish pair in this photo are guarding their eggs.

Freshwater angelfish stay together as a pair for life. After mating, the female lays 100 - 1,000 eggs on a leaf.

Eggs

A male emperor angelfish lives with up to five female mates. If the male dies, one of the females turns into a male fish and becomes the leader of the group!

Emperor angelfish live on coral reefs.

What is a life cycle?

A life cycle is all the different **stages** and changes that a plant or animal goes through in its life. The diagrams on these pages show examples of fish life cycles.

This is a pair of red flower horn fish. There are about 32,500 different types of fish.

A pair of lionfish

1

An adult male and female fish meet. Some fish make a nest.

FISH LIFE CYCLE
Many fish have a life cycle with these stages.

4 **Baby salmon**

Fertilised fish eggs **2**

The female fish lays her eggs. The male fish covers the eggs with a liquid from his body that contains sperm. Now the eggs are fertilised.

Baby fish called fry hatch from the eggs. The tiny babies take care of themselves. They have a yolk sack which they use as food.

3 **A pair of angelfish**

Some fish care for their eggs. Others leave them to hatch on their own.

1

A pair of nurse sharks

An adult male and female shark meet and mate.

3

2

SHARK LIFE CYCLE
Some sharks have a life cycle with these stages.

A black tip shark pup

A female lemon shark and pups

As soon as they are born, the pups are self-sufficient. They have teeth and are ready to hunt.

The female shark gives birth to up to 20 pups at the same time.

Seahorse

Lionfish

Amazing fish life cycles

In this book we are going to find out about some amazing life cycles – from tiny seahorses to colourful lionfish.

Deepsea anglerfish

Anglerfish live at the very bottom of deep oceans where it is very dark. The female has a long spine which comes out of her head. On the end is a ball that can glow like a light.

The female anglerfish can open her mouth really wide to eat fish the same size as her.

The female anglerfish uses her light to attract other fish – then she eats them!

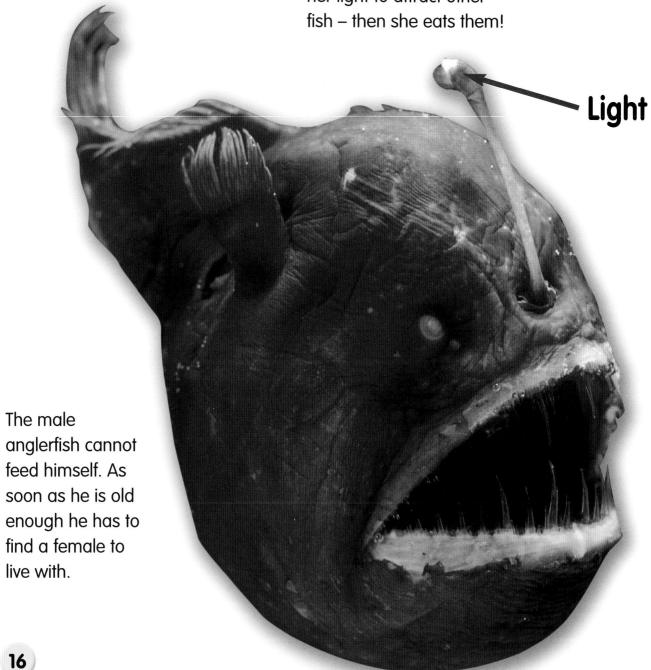

Light

The male anglerfish cannot feed himself. As soon as he is old enough he has to find a female to live with.

The small male attaches
himself to a female.
They stay together for
life. The male gets
smaller and smaller.

Female

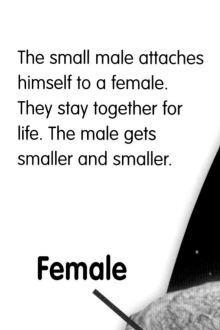

Male

When it is time to reproduce
and lay eggs, the female
already has her mate with her.

A salmon who is ready
to reproduce is called
a spawner.

Salmon

Adult salmon live in the oceans. In the autumn, when it is time to mate and lay eggs, they have to swim back to the freshwater river where they were born.

The salmon have a dangerous journey. They have to swim a long way and they swim **upstream** which is very tiring.

AMAZING FISH FACT
The salmon have to leap up waterfalls and avoid predators such as grizzly bears.

Grizzly bears

Salmon

When a female salmon reaches the spawning ground she makes a nest called a redd and lays up to several thousand eggs. After one or more males fertilise the eggs, the female covers them with gravel and moves on to make another redd.

Thousands of salmon gather in the same place.

The eggs hatch after about four months. The small salmon are called alevins. They have an orange yolk sack which contains all the food they need for the early stages of growth.

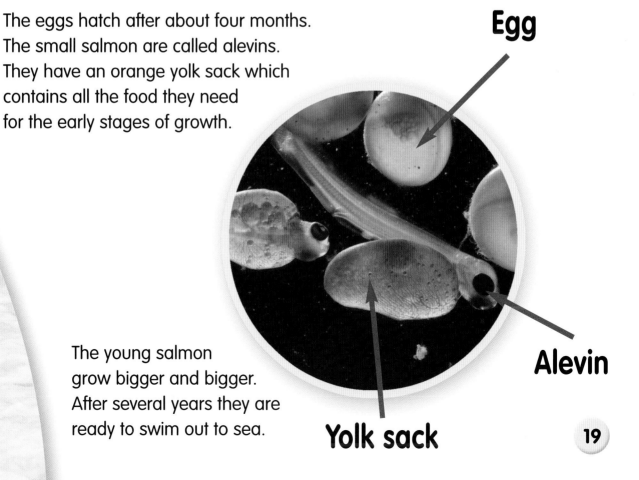

Egg

Alevin

The young salmon grow bigger and bigger. After several years they are ready to swim out to sea.

Yolk sack

Stickleback

Sticklebacks are tiny fish – they grow to just five centimetres long. Some sticklebacks live in saltwater close to the coast. Others live in freshwater ponds, lakes and rivers.

Sticklebacks feed on tiny shellfish and the fry and eggs of other fish.

Nest

Between March and August the male three-spined stickleback changes colour to attract a mate.

Then the male stickleback builds a nest from bits of plant. He does a zigzag dance in front of the nest to attract a female.

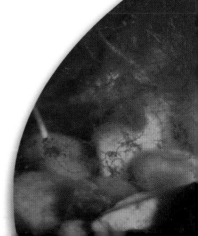

During the mating season, the underside of the male's body becomes a bright orange-red colour, his eyes turn blue and silver scales appear on his back.

Lots of different females lay their eggs in the male's nest. Then he fertilises them.

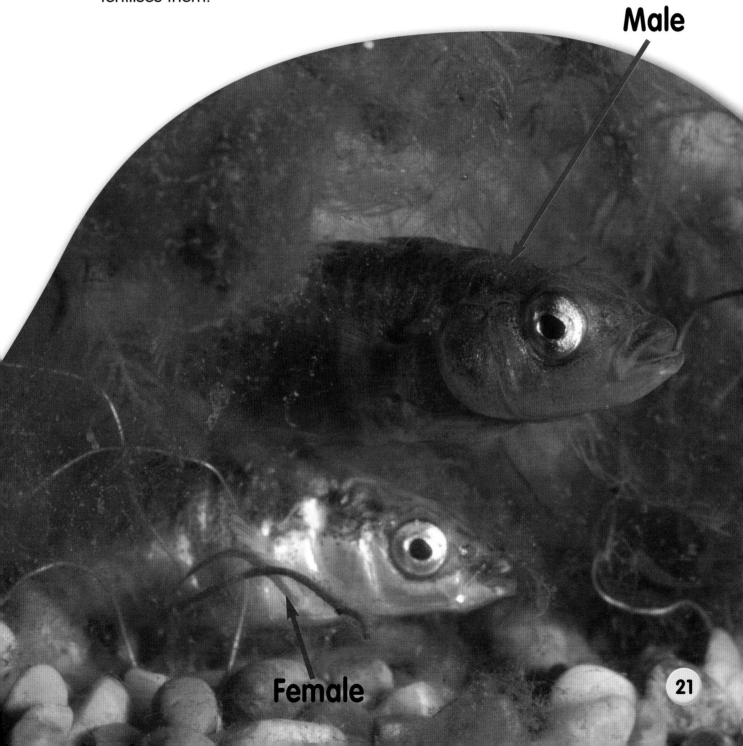

Male

Female

Dogfish

Dogfish live in the ocean. They are a type of small shark. Adult dogfish are about one metre long. They spend most of their time on the seabed hunting for crabs, prawns and small fish.

Dogfish, and other sharks such as this one, have a skeleton made of cartilage. This is the bendy stuff your ears are made of.

After mating, the female dogfish lays her eggs. Each egg is in its own little leathery case.

This is a pair of lesser spotted dogfish.

The female attaches the egg cases to pieces of seaweed so that they do not float away or get damaged. The baby dogfish growing inside the case is called an embryo.

Depending on the temperature of the water, the embryo will stay in the case for up to one year. As it grows it curls around the inside of its egg case.

The egg cases are full of food for the embryo to eat.

By the time the baby dogfish is ready to hatch it will be about 10 centimetres long – twice as long as its egg case.

Egg case

Embryo

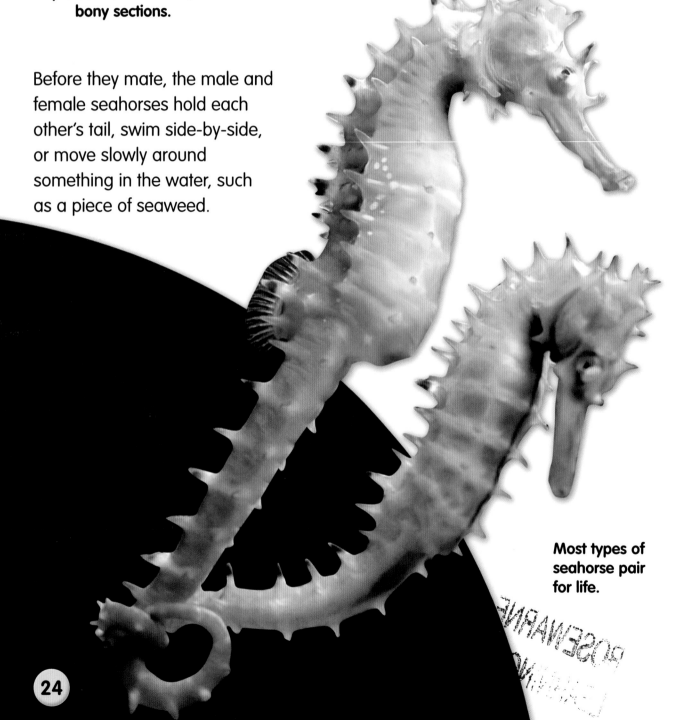

The seahorse's body is covered in armoured plates made of hard, bony sections.

Seahorse

This very unusual looking fish has a horse-like head and a tail it can use to hold onto things. The seahorse can move each of its eyes separately – one can look forwards while the other looks backwards.

Before they mate, the male and female seahorses hold each other's tail, swim side-by-side, or move slowly around something in the water, such as a piece of seaweed.

Most types of seahorse pair for life.

The male seahorse has a pouch on his tummy. The pouch is a bit like a pocket. The female lays her eggs inside the pouch and the male seahorse carries the eggs.

When the babies hatch, the male moves them out of the pouch and into the water. To do so, he holds onto a piece of seaweed with his long tail. He rocks backwards and forwards until the babies pop out of his pouch. This can last from 12 hours to 2 days.

Baby seahorse   Pouch

AMAZING FISH FACT
Some seahorses can change colour to match their surroundings.

ROSEWARNE LEARNING CENTRE

**Lionfish live on coral
reefs in warm seas.**

Lionfish

Adult lionfish usually live alone, but when they are ready to mate they get together in groups of three to eight. For three or four days each male will try to get a female to notice him.

Sometimes the males will fight. They bite each other and ram each other with their spiky fins.

**AMAZING
FISH FACT**
The lionfish's needle-like fins can give a predator a poisonous sting.

Fins

Adult lionfish are 30 – 40 centimetres long.

When the male has found a partner, the two fish swim face to face and turn around in circles. They dance to the surface of the water.

On the surface of the water the female lays a ball of thousands of eggs. When the male has fertilised the eggs, the parents leave. After about three months the eggs hatch.

Baby lionfish

After hatching, the baby lionfish sink to the seabed to hide away from predators, such as bigger fish.

Some adult
hammerheads are three
to four metres long.

Hammerhead shark

Hammerhead sharks live in warm parts of
the Pacific, Indian and Atlantic Oceans.
They are strong swimmers and have
been known to attack people!

Dorsal fin

The hammerhead
shark has eyes at each
end of its wide head.
Scientists believe
having eyes like this
might help the shark
to see all around it
when it is hunting.

Gill slits

Depending on the species, the female hammerhead shark gives birth to between 6 and 31 pups at a time.

The pups may be up to 70 centimetres long when they are born. They look like small versions of the adults. The pups have to look after themselves as soon as they are born.

Eye

Hammerhead sharks eat fish and other sharks. Stingrays are their favourite food.

AMAZING FISH FACT

Some sharks have several rows of very sharp teeth. When a tooth falls out, it is replaced with a tooth from the row behind it.

Stingray

That's amazing!

Many of the pictures in this book were taken using a special underwater camera.

All fish big or small use their gills to breathe underwater. If humans want to spend time underwater studying fish life cycles and photographing them we have to wear diving suits and breathe oxygen from a tank.

AMAZING FISH FACT
The sunfish can grow to over three metres long, and can weigh up to 2,300 kilograms.

Sunfish

A female sunfish can lay 300 million eggs each year. Each egg is smaller than a fullstop.

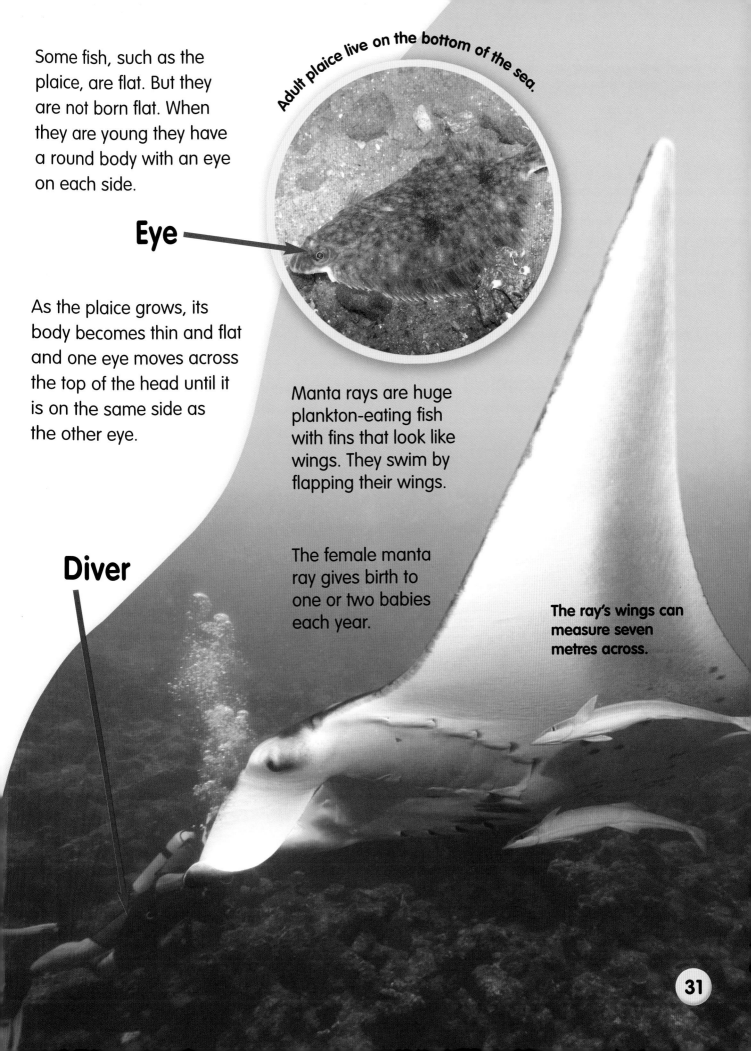

Some fish, such as the plaice, are flat. But they are not born flat. When they are young they have a round body with an eye on each side.

Eye

As the plaice grows, its body becomes thin and flat and one eye moves across the top of the head until it is on the same side as the other eye.

Manta rays are huge plankton-eating fish with fins that look like wings. They swim by flapping their wings.

Diver

The female manta ray gives birth to one or two babies each year.

The ray's wings can measure seven metres across.

Glossary

camouflage – Colours, marks or a shape that hides an animal from its predators, and the animals it hunts.

coral reefs – Underwater places made from the hard, external skeletons of coral animals called polyps. When a polyp dies, its skeleton stays as part of the reef, so the reef gets bigger and bigger.

freshwater – Rainwater, and the water in ponds and some rivers. It is not salty.

gills – Breathing organs (parts of the body) of fish and many other animals that live in water.

mate – When a male and female animal meet and have babies.

oxygen – A gas that most animals need for life.

plankton – Tiny animals and plants that live in oceans and lakes. They are so small you need a microscope to see them.

predators – Animals which hunt and kill other animals for food.

reproduce – To have babies.

saltwater – Water with salt in it, including the water found in oceans and some lakes.

scales – Small, overlapping sections of hard skin that cover the bodies of fish.

sea anemones – An ocean animal with stinging tentacles – it looks like a plant!

stages – Different times of an animal's life when the animal changes.

swamps – Wet lowland areas where water collects and many water plants grow.

upstream – The opposite direction to the flow of water in a river or stream.

Index